A Wonderful Catastrophe

Colette Love Hilliard

ISBN-10: 0-9966243-5-X

ISBN-13: 978-0-9966243-5-0

Author: Colette Love Hilliard

Editors: Richard J. Heby & Mark Danowsky

Wood & Water Press

350 W53rd Street, #4i

New York, NY 10019

United States

Quantity sales. Special discounts are available on quantity purchases. For details, contact the publisher by email at editor@beechwoodreview.com.

Printed in the United States of America.

www.woodandwater.press

Dedication

For my husband because this journey is ours.

Contents

1 .... Promise

2 .... Unpacking

3 .... Relief

4 .... Solitary

5 .... Collapse

6 .... Folds

7 .... Worn

8 .... Echo

9 .... Mother

10 .... Reason

11 .... Troubled

12 .... Consolation

13 .... Through

14 .... Grief

15 .... Words

16 .... In between

17 .... Catastrophe

18 .... Endure

19 .... Official

20 .... Remember

21 .... Love

22 .... Courage

23 .... Undone

24 .... Close

25 .... Worst

26 .... Entrance

27 .... Miraculous

28	....	Infinity
29	....	Agony
30	....	Silence
31	....	Avalanche
32	....	Conflicted
33	....	Cruel
34	....	Struck
35	....	Hope
36	....	Impossibility
37	....	Fault
38	....	Why
39	....	Science
40	....	Can't
41	....	Hurt
42	....	Glass
43	....	Over
44	....	Try
45	....	Apologies
46	....	Forget
47	....	Loss
48	....	Reopen
49	....	Reconciled
50	....	Forgive
51	....	Haunted
52	....	Uncovered
53	....	Unafraid
54	....	Storm
55	....	Road
56	....	Unpaved

Introduction

I didn't set out to become an artist or a poet. I wanted to be a mother, actually. So far, though, I've only been able to create new life out of old books in the form of found poetry. This book is born out of love as much as devastation. It is the story of my infertility journey. Every piece is an attempt to rationalize the experience—an attempt to heal the wounds no one can see. I share them with you here, in this collection, because I know I am one of many grappling with this isolating disease, and it is my hope that my work will inspire others to create something beautiful out of something broken.

Editor's Note

Pause a moment. Before you read and inevitably re-read, notice the backdrop, recognize the context. Blackout poetry, aka erasure, is a type of found poetry, which involves crossing out, drawing over, or otherwise "erasing" part of a text, to create a new work. Erasure is often inspirational, poetic, or narrative. In the case of *A Wonderful Catastrophe*, it's all three. Enjoy.

x

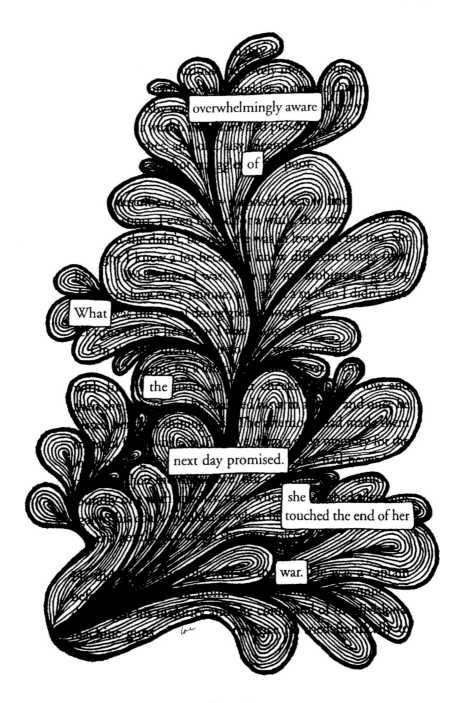

overwhelmingly aware of What the next day promised. she touched the end of her war.

Promise

1

she took a deep breath. and began unpacking Her heart

Unpacking

2

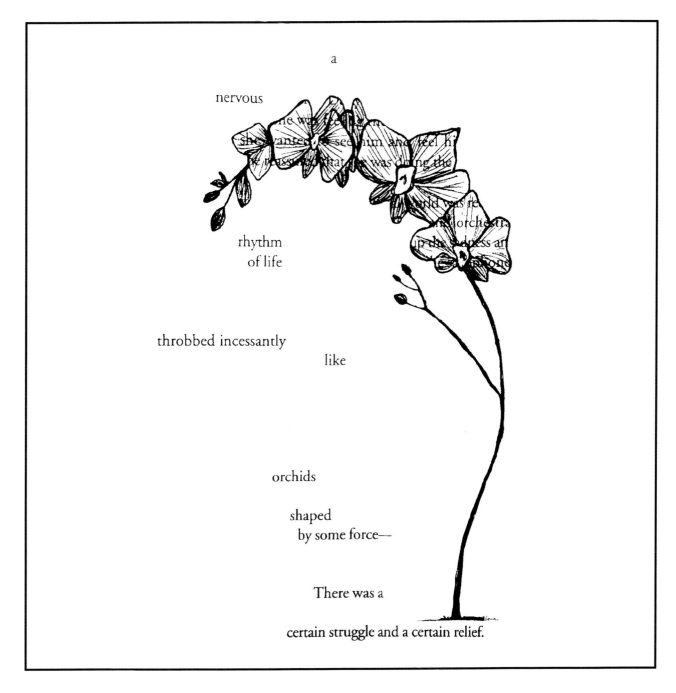

a

nervous

rhythm
of life

throbbed incessantly

like

orchids

shaped
by some force—

There was a

certain struggle and a certain relief.

Relief
—
3

Cursed, cursed be the fiend that brought misery on his grey hairs, and doomed him to waste in wretchedness! He could not live under the horrors that were accumulated around him; the springs of existence suddenly gave way: he was unable to rise from his bed, and in a few days he died in my arms.

What then became of me? I know not; I lost sensation, and chains and darkness were the only objects that pressed upon me. Sometimes, indeed, I dreamt that I wandered in flowery meadows and pleasant vales with the friends of my youth; but I awoke, and found myself in a dungeon. Melancholy followed, but by degrees I gained a clear conception of my miseries and situation, and was then released from my prison. For they had called me mad; and during many months, as I understood, a solitary cell had been my habitation.

Liberty, however, had been an useless gift to me, had I not, as I awakened to reason, at the same time awakened to revenge. As the memory of past misfortunes pressed upon me, I began to reflect on their cause — the monster whom I had created, the miserable dæmon whom I had sent abroad into the world for my destruction. I was possessed by a maddening rage when I thought of him, and desired and ardently prayed that I might have him within my grasp to wreak a great and signal revenge on his cursed head.

Nor did my hate long confine itself to useless wishes; I began to reflect on the best means of securing him; and, for this purpose, about a month after my release, I repaired to a criminal judge in the town, and told him that I had an accusation to make; that I knew the destroyer of my family; and that I required him to exert his whole authority for the apprehension of the murderer.

The magistrate listened to me with attention and kindness: —"Be assured, sir," said he, "no pains or exertions on my part shall be spared to discover the villain."

"I thank you," replied I; "listen, therefore, to the deposition that I have to make. It is indeed a tale so strange, that I should fear you would not credit it, were there not something in truth which, however wonderful, forces conviction. The story is too connected to be mistaken for a dream, and I have no motive for falsehood." My manner, as I thus addressed him, was impressive, but calm; I had formed in my own heart a resolution to pursue my destroyer to death; and this purpose quieted my agony, and for an interval reconciled me to life. I now related my

Solitary

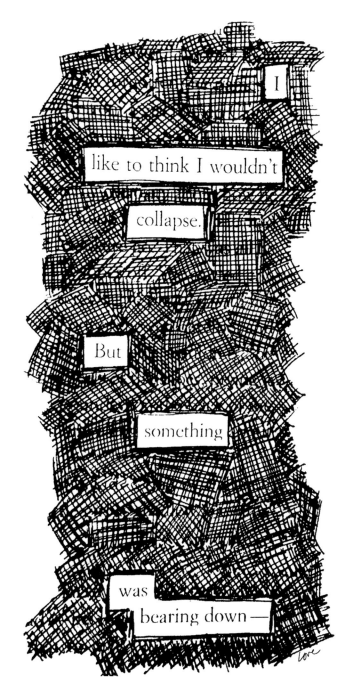

I

like to think I wouldn't

collapse.

But

something

was

bearing down—

Collapse

5

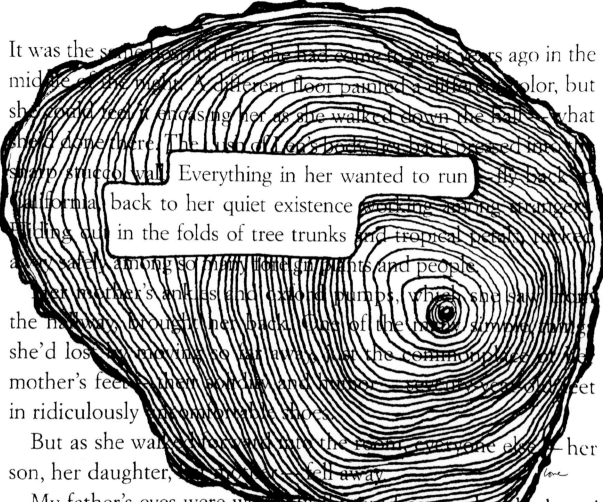

It was the same hospital that she had come to eight years ago in the middle of the night. A different floor painted a different color, but she could feel it encasing her as she walked down the hall. In what she'd done there. The cushion on's back, her back pressed into the sharp stucco wall. Everything in her wanted to run — fly back to California, back to her quiet existence working among strangers, hiding out in the folds of tree trunks and tropical petals, tucked away safe, among so many foreign plants and people.

Her mother's ankles and oxford pumps, which she saw from the hallway, brought her back. One of the many simple things she'd lost by moving so far away — that the commonplace of her mother's feet — their solidity and humor — seventy-year-old feet in ridiculously uncomfortable shoes.

But as she walked forward into the room, everyone else — her son, her daughter, her mother — fell away.

My father's eyes were weak but flickered open when he heard her enter. He had tubes and wires coming out of his wrist and shoulder. His head seemed so fragile on the small square pillow.

She held his hand and cried silently, letting the tears come freely.

Folds

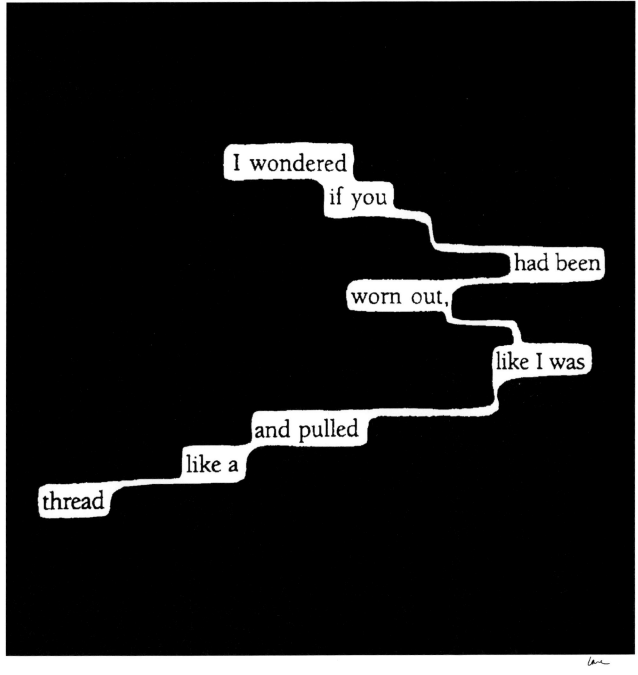

Worn

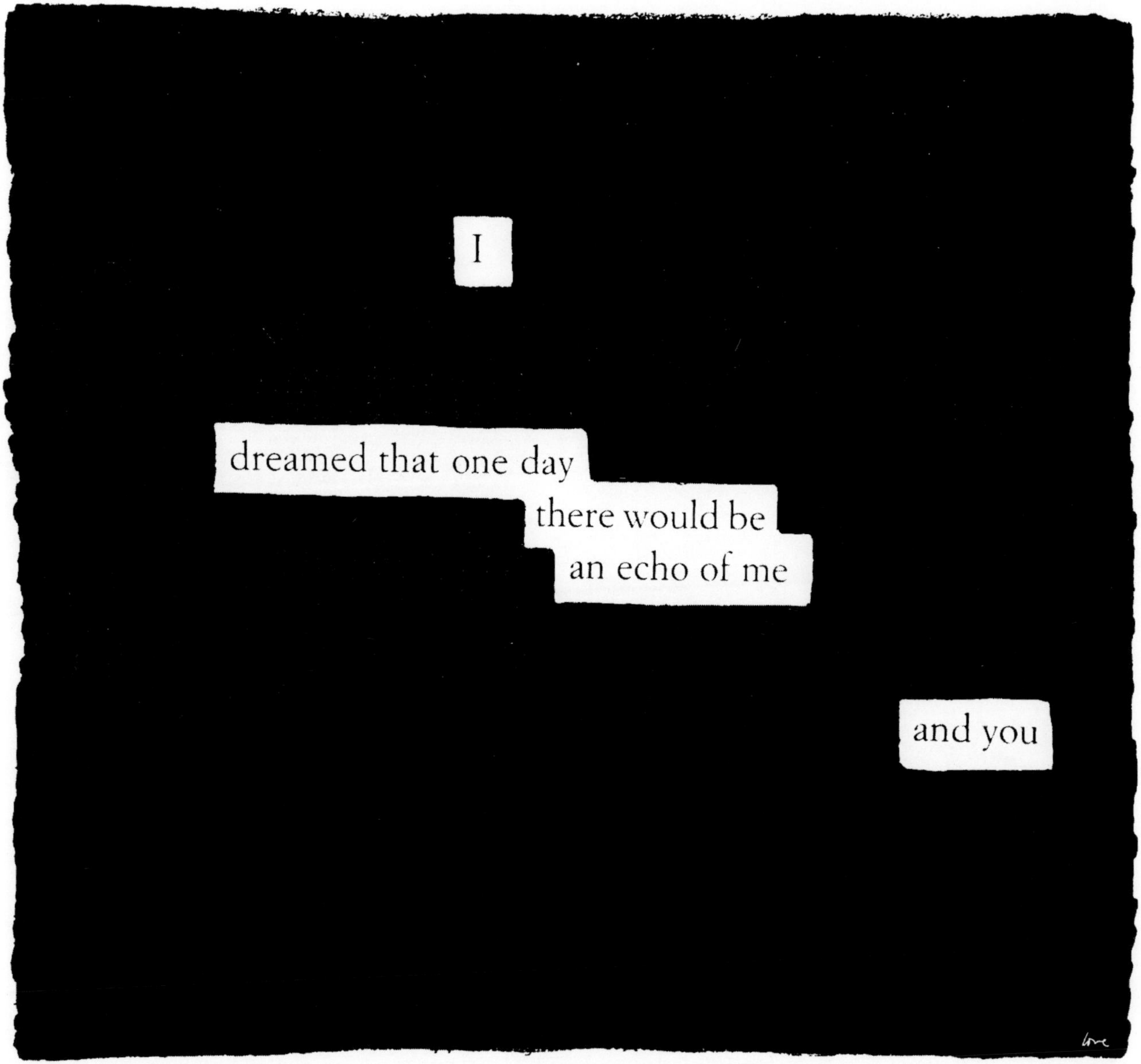

I

dreamed that one day
there would be
an echo of me

and you

Echo

8

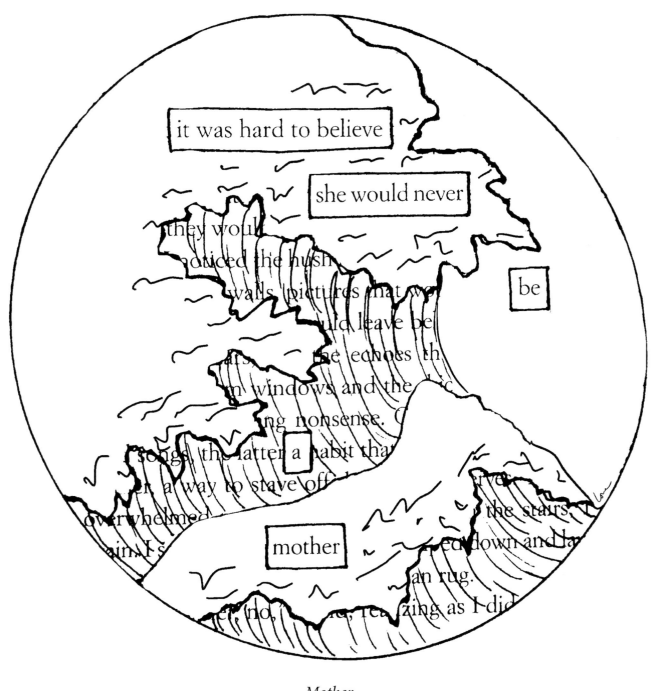

it was hard to believe

she would never

be

mother

Mother

to reason,
is
maddening

Reason

10

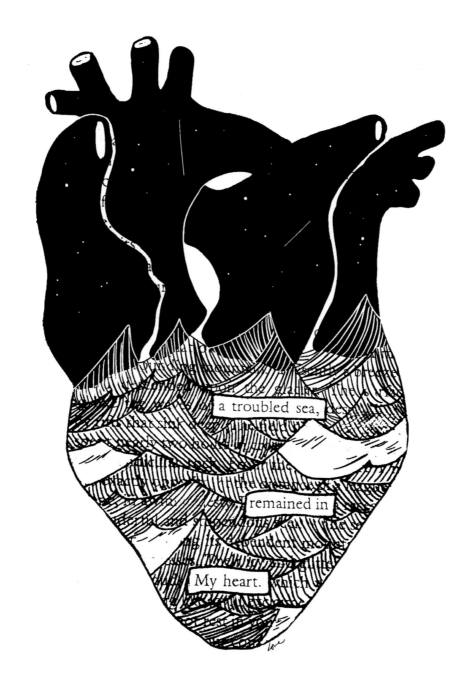

a troubled sea,

remained in

My heart.

Troubled

I had

a

sense of guilt,
such as no language can describe.

my only consolation —

his serene

love

Consolation

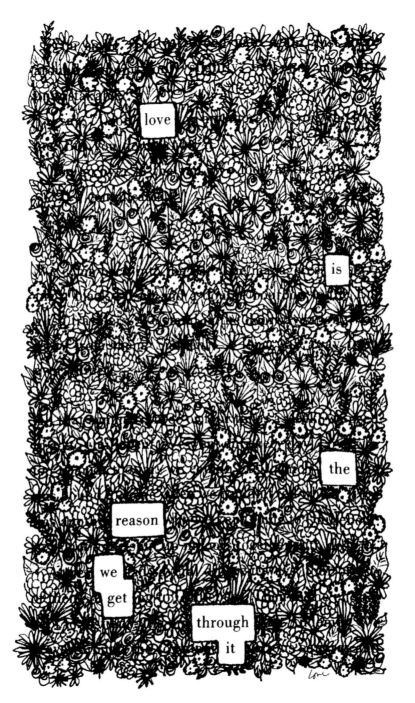

love

is

the

reason

we
get

through
it

Through

she

thought

of

the kisses
like

whispers calling her away from
grief.

Everything will fall into place.

The words so simple and true. They speak to me, pacify me. Although I am no expert on this weird beautiful life I let the sounds slow and soft carry me carry me.

Words

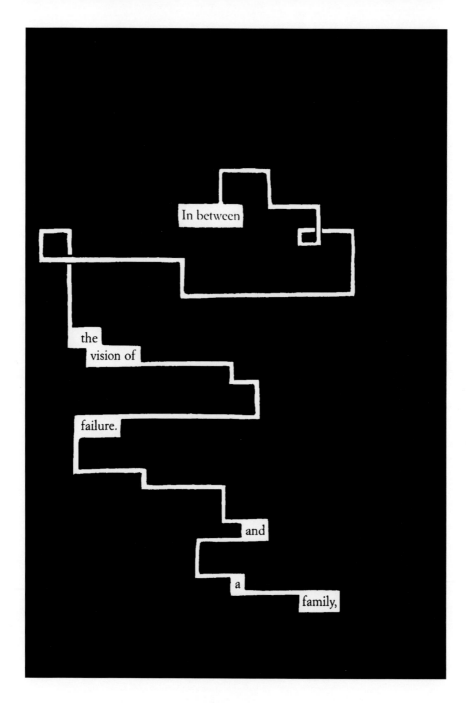

In between

16

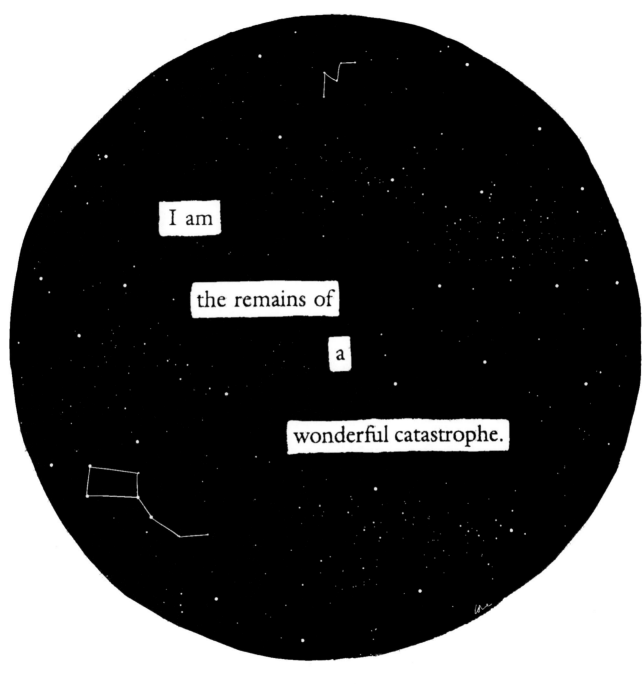

I am

the remains of

a

wonderful catastrophe.

Catastrophe

I may one day

be surprised at
what I have endured.

Endure

miraculous
waves
of

wonder

climbed
around her
and
the

desire to

start over again

was

official

Official

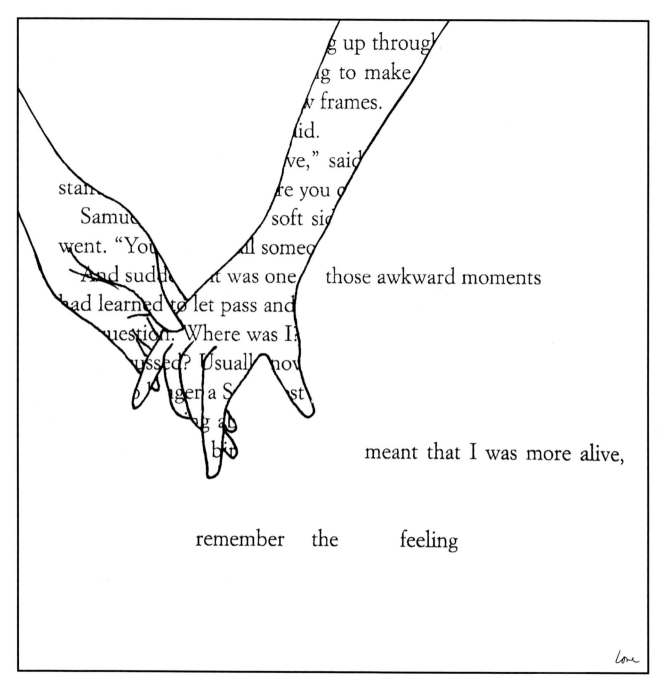

those awkward moments

meant that I was more alive,

remember   the   feeling

Love

Remember

———

20

"I love you," Samuel said.

I love you,

I love you, and I want to

"Not for me it isn't," my sister said.

Samuel got up off the floor where he had

sister, and went to his knees in front of her. "

Samuel

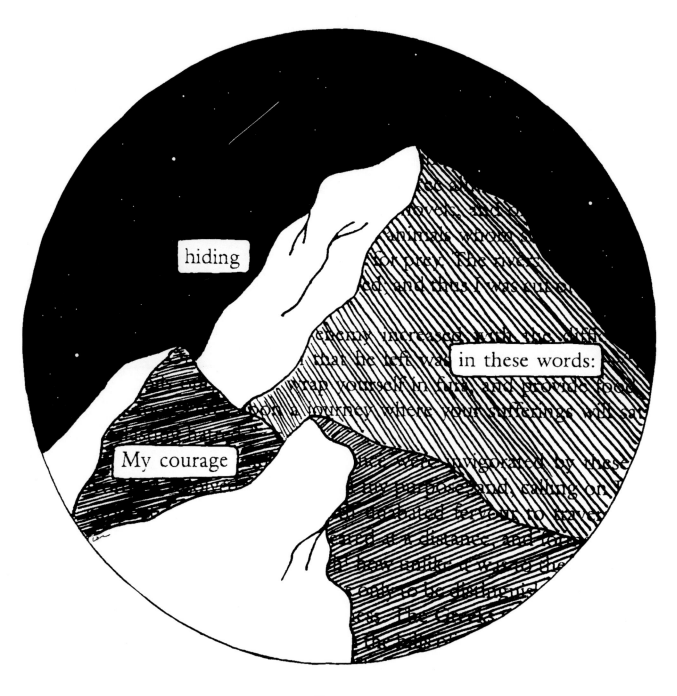

Courage

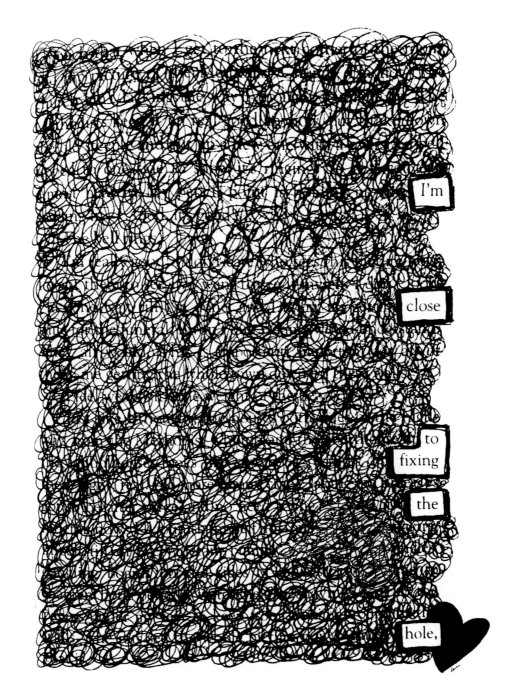

I'm

close

to fixing

the

hole,

Close

—

24

y bastard of a
y divorce and he's t
e's not what you would call a
as tractable as a totem pole. I look
I saw myself. . . ." Matthew took a long
He had made it through the worst part. the lie was
and he saw that Maggie was eager to believe him. "I
I want you to help me be more of a person. It's a
some hell of a nerve on you

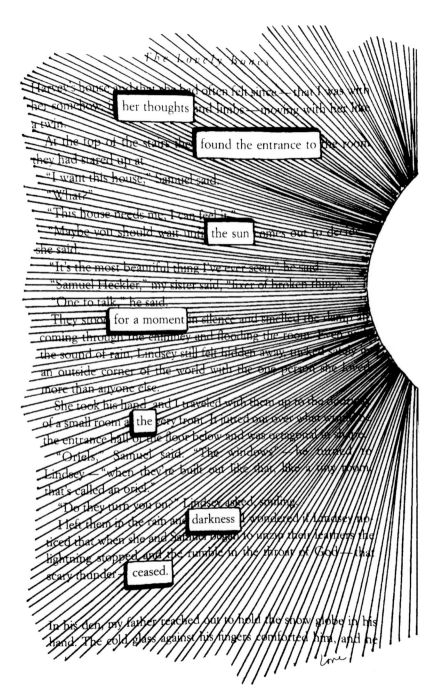

Entrance

26

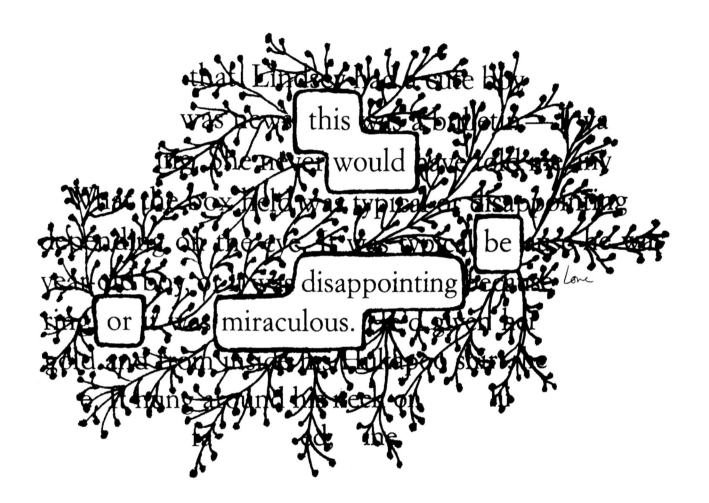

this would be

disappointing or miraculous.

Miraculous

27

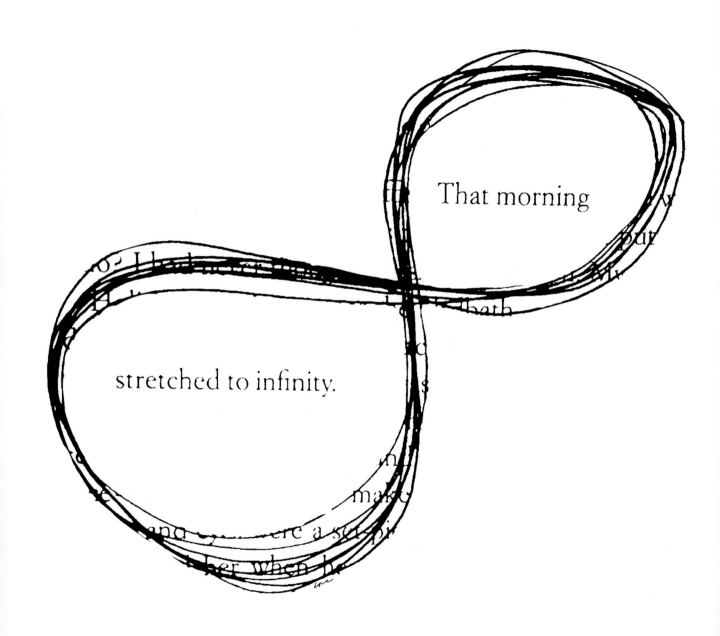

That morning

stretched to infinity.

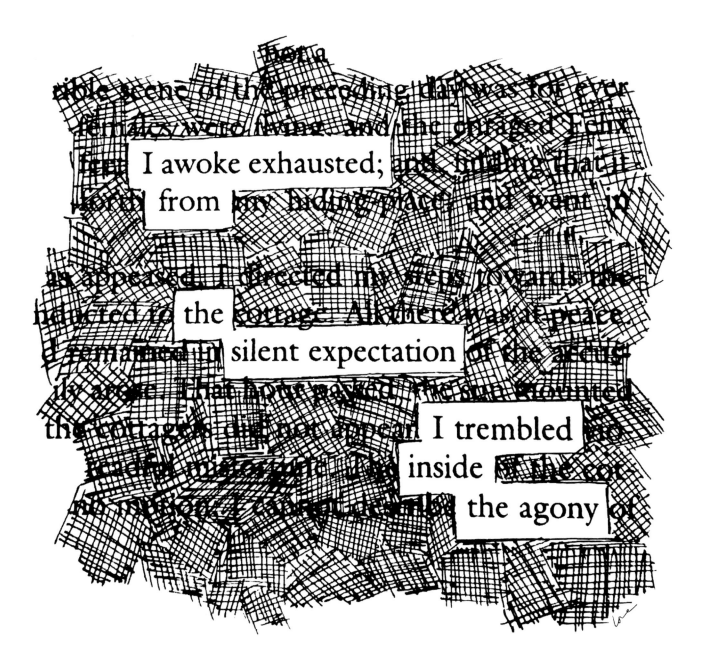

I awoke exhausted; and from the silent expectation I trembled inside the agony

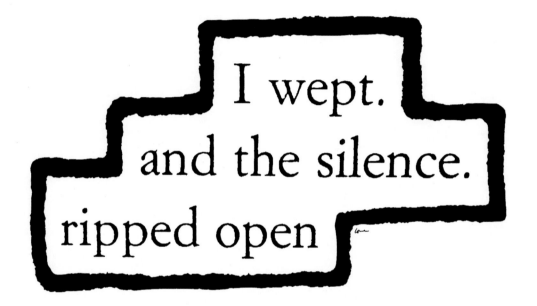

I wept.
and the silence.
ripped open

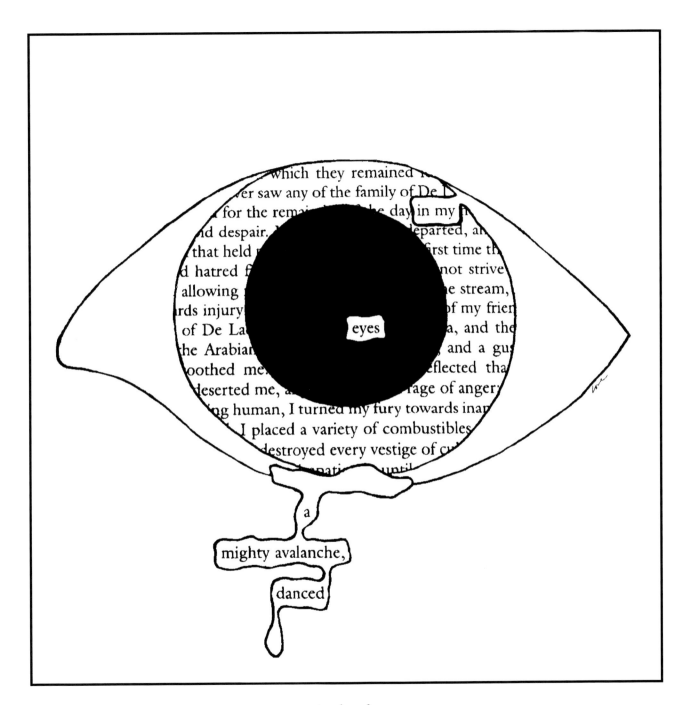

Avalanche

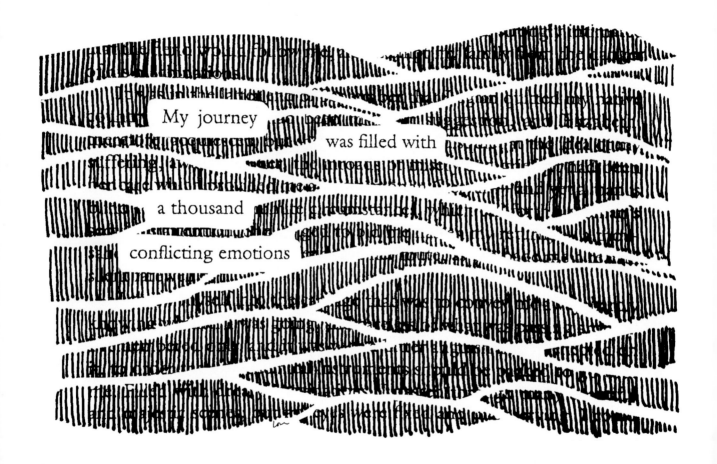

My journey was filled with a thousand conflicting emotions

Conflicted

"Nothing is ever certain,"

rang in her ears again.

It was

a cruel phrase that preyed

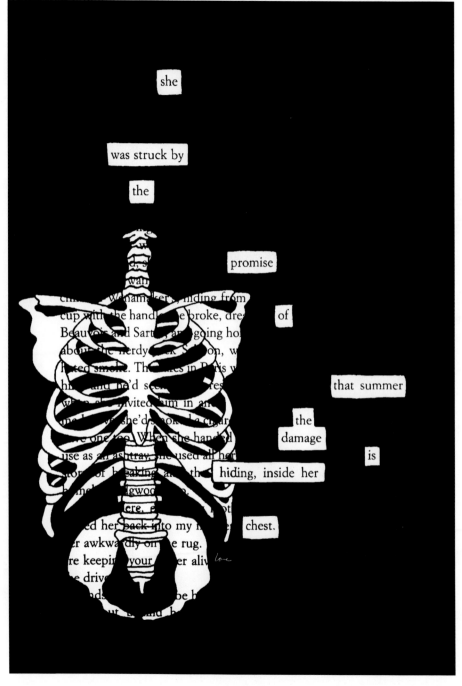

she

was struck by

the

promise

of

that summer

the
damage

is

hiding, inside her

chest.

Struck
———
34

Nothing is so painful as hope snatched away;

Hope

35

sse I my m
s around the
makeup. She wo as
no everyone was, whe ther or n
e of their house, what the usban
hey drove. She made a soli analog of th
a way, I now realized, to try to n erstand h
A miscalculated circling, a sad, par erless dan
k-y," my grandmother said as she ap roa hed my
front porch, "we need some stiff drinks She saw L
ying to sneak up the stairs and gain few ore m
re the required visitation. "Kid hates me," Grandm
Her smile was frozen, her teeth per ect and white.
Mother," my mother said. And I wanted to rush into tho
ean eyes of loss. "I'm sure Lindsey s just going to make he
esentable."

"A impossibility n this house!" sa my grandmother.

"Lynn," said my father, "thi s a dif ren house than last time
you were here. I'll get you a rink, ut I ask ou to respe t at."

"Still handsome as hell, ack," my randmother said

My mother took my grandmother's coat. Holiday had been
closed up in my father's den a soon as Buckley had yelled from
his post at the upstairs window "It's Grandma!" My other
bragged to Nate or anyone w o would listen that his rand
mother had the biggest cars in the w ole wide world.

"You look lovely, Mother," my other said

"Hmmmm." While my father wa out of earsh t, my rand
mother said, "How is he?"

"We're all coping, but it's hard.

"Is he still muttering about that man hav ng done it?"

"He still thinks so, yes."

"You'll be sued you know," she aid.

"He hasn't told anyone but the po ce."

Impossibility

———

36

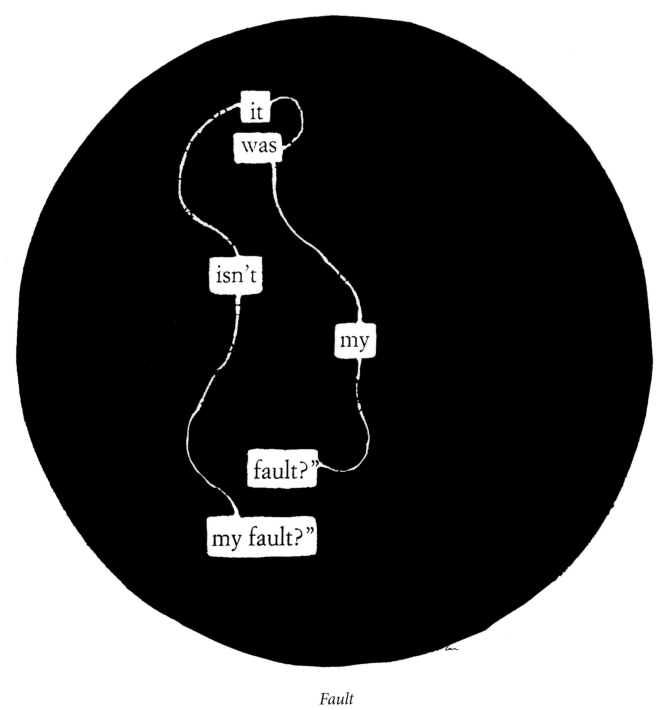

Fault

37

...man who... before to... time ask... His... smiles and... to addiction. The women and... from then the question start to flow that... something horrible. Why does... that way. Because we know what we're going to do... and we... to you and we... do it. What does it... like when you want... Need, overwhelming need, uncontrollable need, unimaginable need. What does it feel like when you... relief followed by... followed by more need. Why can't you stop? I don't know. Why can't you stop? I don't know. Why can't you stop? I don't know.

There are other, simpler, more technical questions. What is crack and how do you use it? Crack is cocaine cooked... with... baking powder... a rock... Where do you buy it and how much does it cost? You buy it... It is... What is meth and how is it made? Meth is... cooking... also called... for... sometimes pink or... and... powder. What does it do to you? Rob you of... your heart, rob you of your soul, take away... money, and... you to sleep, rob you of your sanity.

...questions... Unlike the family members, we already know the answers. We

Love

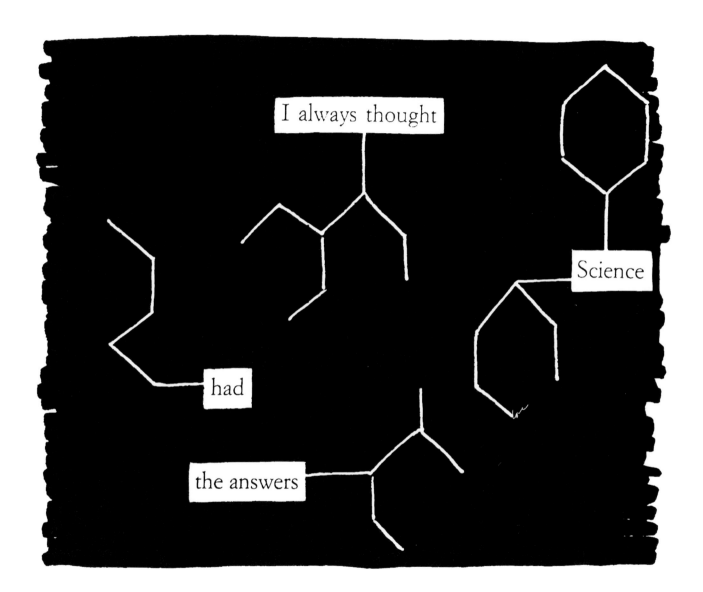

Science
—
39

"I want to grow up and have babies.

"But

I can't

Can't

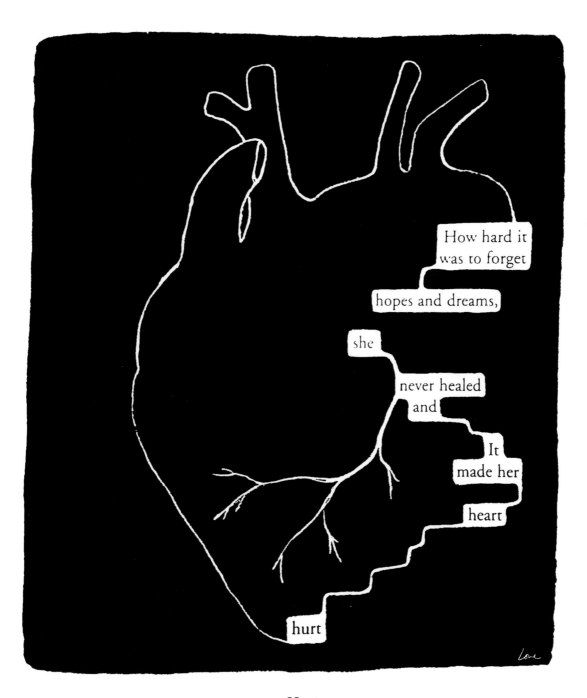

Hurt

41

had sag... ...years. Then...

...week before my death.

...e first.

...He turned and saw all the

My heart

years they ma... ...hands that had b... them

ther's, his dead child's. I wat... ...smash

christened the walls and woo... ...th the n...

and afterward he stood in... ...st room/de...

...een glass. The bottles, a... ...em, lay bro...

...boat bodies stre... among them

piece of glass, ...every shard

...and arou...

...st for...

...t, an...

...of...

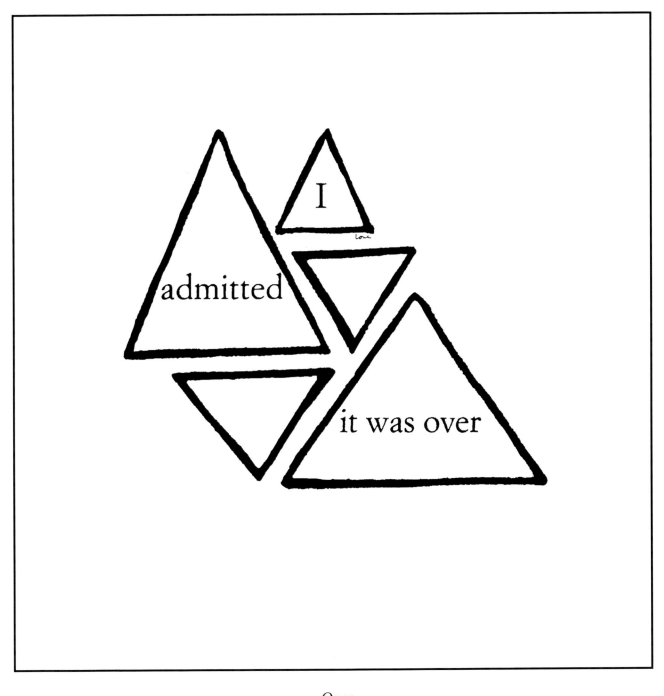

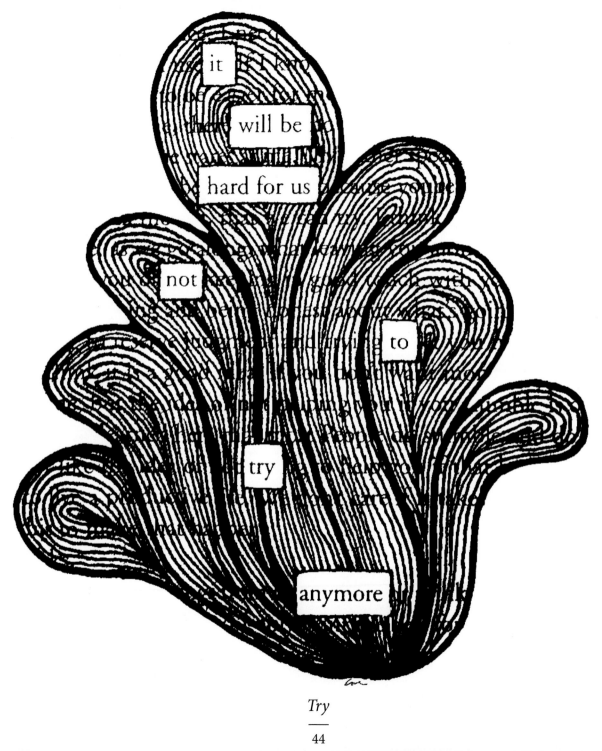

it
will be
hard for us
not
to
try
anymore

Try

44

these

apologetic whispers.

grow

heavy   inside her

Apologies

45

I listen to the leaves. at the ground. I try to lose myself. I try to forget

and , I try to forget about what lies in front of me. I

try to forget about on and recovery. I try to forget that there is a

that in my head and I try to forget that there is a

World within my head. forget everything.

lose, try to lose. The crack of leaves fades

all stones and the stones lead me to a

delicate sheets of thin, fractured ice. I

beneath, packs of small fish dance, solitary weeds lie still, algae clings to whatever it can find. A shell sits lonely and silent and I stop and I watch it. Somewhere within there is life. At some point life will shed its shell and reemerge. I stare at the shell in the shallows beneath a delicate sheet of fractures. Life reemerging. I want to forget, but I can't.

I walk again, continue to try, continue continue. The shore drifts into a wide stretch of tall, dead, yellow grass and my feet become silent on an artery of hard, black, packed dirt. As they carry me through the grass, I run my hands along the sharp frozen tips of the grass and they tickle me and I laugh and the sound of my laughter calms me. Forget, lose, forget, please lose. It tickles me and I laugh.

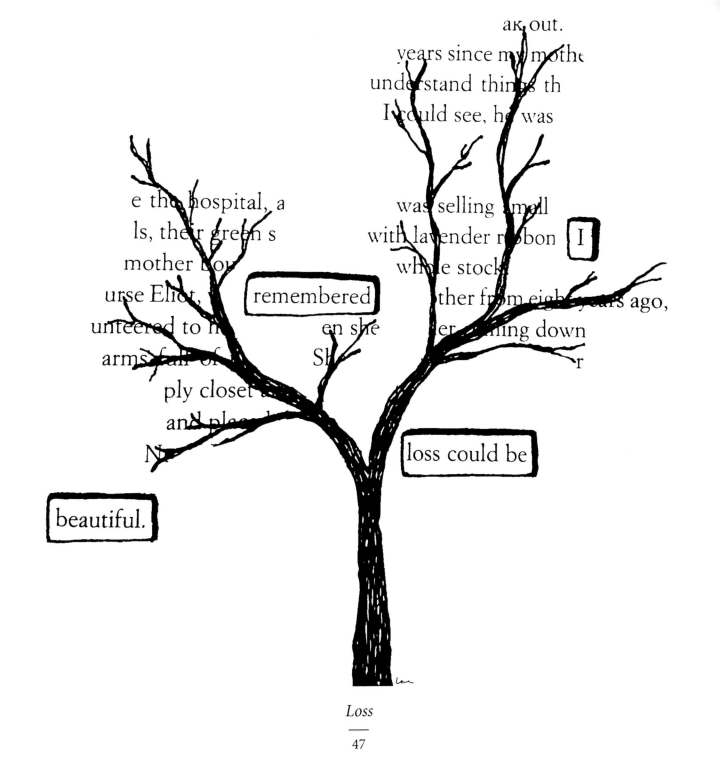

ak out.
years since my mothe
understand things th
I could see, he was

e the hospital, a
ls, their green s
mother bou
urse Eliot,
unteered to
arms full of
ply closet
and p
N

was selling small
with lavender ribbon   I
whole stock
ther from eight years ago,
en she   ing down
Sh   r

remembered

loss could be

beautiful.

Loss

47

reopen the wound.
you are

poetry.

Reopen

48

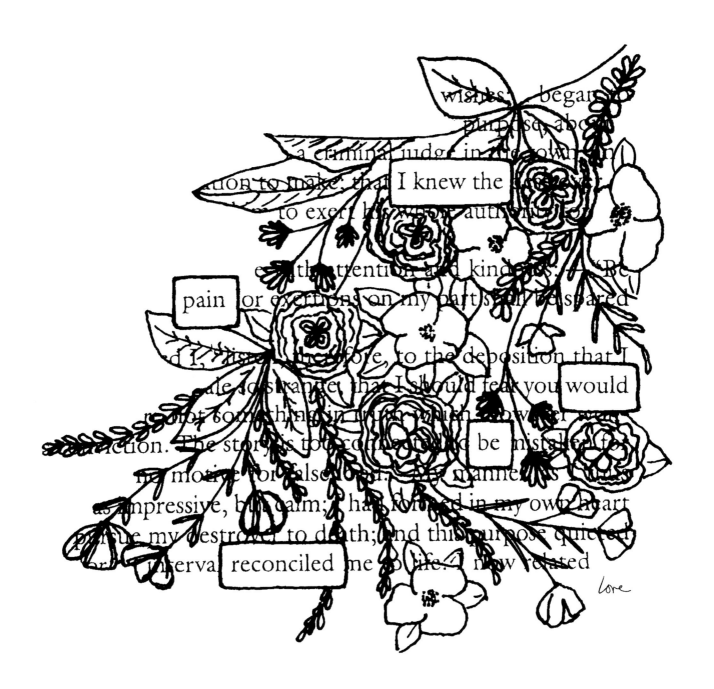

I knew the

pain

would

reconciled

Reconciled

I

"Forgive

myself.

Forgive

50

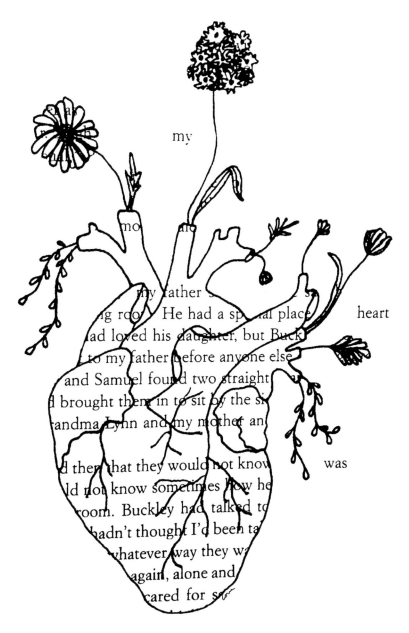

my

heart

my father

g roo   He had a sp   al place

ad loved his daughter, but Buck

to my father before anyone else

and Samuel found two straight

brought them in to sit by the si

andma Lynn and my mother an

d then that they would not know   was

ld not know sometimes how he

room. Buckley had talked to

hadn't thought I'd been ta

whatever way they w

again, alone and

cared for s

no longer

haunted.

Haunted

Uncovered

one else had. She didn't know what she would do with *love*
taking copious notes for the future, but she had grow unafraid
The world she saw of dead women and children
real to her as the world in which she lived.

In the library at Penn, Ray read about bold-
face heading "The Conditions of Death. a study
done in nursing homes in which a large percent of ients re-
ported to the doctors and nurses that they saw e standing
at the end of their bed at night. Often this person tried to talk to
them or call their name. Sometimes the patients were in such a
high state of agitation during these delusions that they had to be
given a sedative or strapped to their beds.

The text went on to explain that these visions were a result of
small strokes that often preceded death. "What is commonly
thought of by the layman as the Angel of Death, when discussed
at all with the patient's family, should be presented to them as a
small series of strokes compo lready precipitous state
of decline."

For a moment, with his finger marki the ace in the book,
Ray imagined what it would be like if, ver the bed of an
elderly patient, remaining as open could to possibility, he
might feel something brush past him Ruth had so many years
ago in the parking lot.

Mr. Harvey had been l wild within e Northeast Corridor
from the outlying areas of sto he northern tips of the
southern states, where he would go ier work and fewer
questions and make an occasional attempt eform. He had al-
ways liked Pennsylvania and had crisscrossed the long state,
camping sometimes behind the 7-Eleven just down the local high-

Unafraid

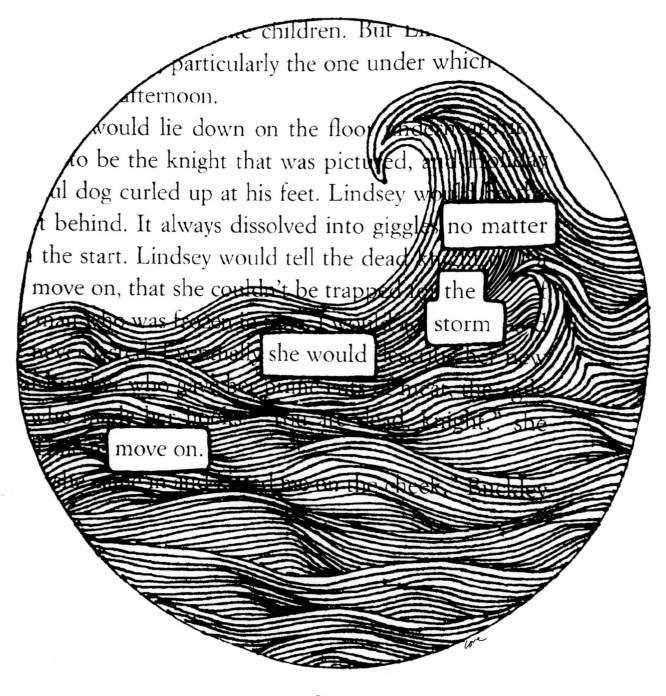

no matter

the

storm

she would

move on.

Storm

They reached the end

of the road.

and began walking

past it.

Road

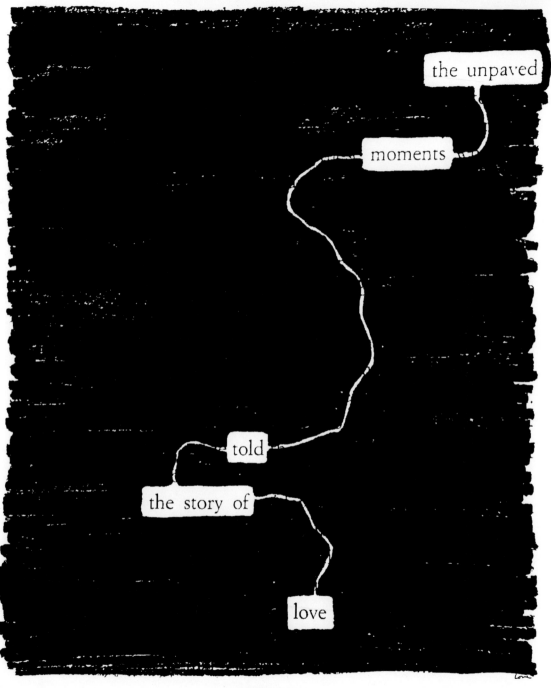

Unpaved